FISH
AND SEAFOOD

Typeset by MATS, Southend-on-Sea, Essex
Printed in Slovenia

Ceres Verlag recipes compiled and translated by
Stephen Challacombe

Cover design by Minkowsky, Enkhuizen,
The Netherlands
JO246 UK

Illustrations by Camilla Sopwith
Edited by Anne Sheasby
ISBN 1 84053 112 6

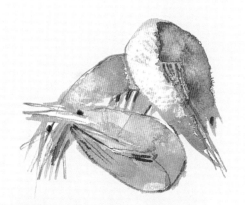

FISH
AND SEAFOOD

EXOTIC AND NUTRITIOUS MEALS TO MAKE IN MINUTES

 **REBO**
PRODUCTIONS

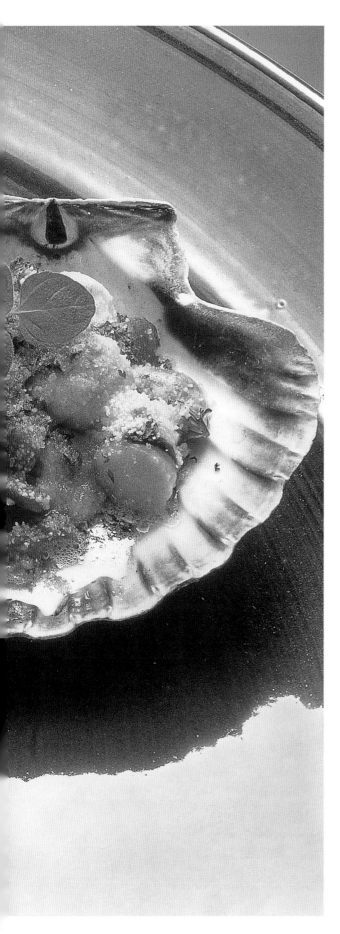

Contents

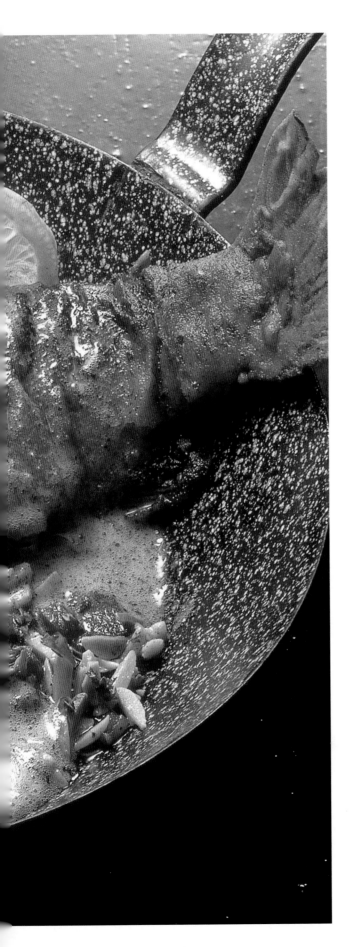

Introduction

Fish and seafood are excellent sources of protein in our diet, and most varieties are also rich in vitamin B12. At the same time, fish is generally very low in fat, and even the oily varieties of fish, such as salmon, trout, mackerel, sardines, herring and anchovies, contain unsaturated fats which, unlike saturated animal fats, can be health-promoting.

It is widely believed that the high levels of omega-3 fatty acids offered by oily fish help to protect the body against heart and circulatory problems, and to reduce the risk of thrombosis. These fatty acids are also considered to be vital to the healthy development of the brain and eyes, and are strongly recommended for women in pregnancy.

Fish and seafood have the added benefits of being quick to cook and easy on the digestive system. They also offer a wide variety of fresh flavours and textures, and are highly versatile in a whole range of dishes. As for added flavourings, most fish and seafood demand a subtle approach, using fresh herbs, fragrant spices and sharp-tasting citrus juices or tomatoes. However, the more robust fish, such as mackerel, red mullet and trout, can be enhanced by stronger seasoning with garlic, peppercorns and chilli. Liquorice-like flavours, provided by fennel and aniseed, are wonderfully complementary of fish and create a sophisticated taste experience.

Fish and seafood form the perfect basis for rich and satisfying soups and stews, and we present a range of inviting recipes to choose from in this special collection, including a contemporary version of the traditional clam chowder of New England fame. Sample other variations on a classical theme, such as Salmon in Mustard Sauce, akin to the Swedish gravadlax, Marinated Raw Fish in the Latin American tradition of ceviche and spiced-up English Potted Shrimps. Besides luscious and exotic salads, fish and shellfish are teamed with pasta, combined with nuts and fruits and served in delicately spiced, creamy sauces, to liven up your everyday repertoire. To help you entertain in high style, we also feature some truly luxurious and unusual dishes – guaranteed to impress your guests, however prestigious the occasion!

Gratin of Scallops

In this special-occasion starter or snack, succulent scallops are baked in their shells with a tomato, onion and fresh herb mixture, topped with a golden, crispy crumb.

Preparation time: 15 minutes • Cooking time: 3-5 minutes • Serves: 4

Ingredients

20 fresh scallops, in their shells	4 sprigs of fresh marjoram, finely chopped
Salt and freshly ground black pepper	85 g (3 oz) fresh white breadcrumbs
2 beefsteak tomatoes	70 g (2½ oz) butter, melted
2 shallots or small onions, chopped	Fresh herb sprigs, to garnish
1 sprig of fresh parsley, finely chopped	

Method

1
Remove the scallops from their shells and blanch for 1 minute in a saucepan of boiling salted water.

2
Drain, then divide between 4 scallop shells or portion-sized ovenproof plates. Season to taste with salt and pepper.

3
Cut crosses in the tops of the tomatoes and plunge into a bowl of boiling water for about 20 seconds, then plunge into cold water.

4
Remove from the water, drain, then remove and discard the skins.

5
Cut the tomatoes in half, remove and discard the hard cores and seeds, then slice the flesh into small chunks.

6
Scatter the tomatoes, shallots or onions, herbs and breadcrumbs over the scallops. Drizzle the butter over each portion.

8
Cook in a preheated oven at 200°C/400°F/Gas Mark 6 for 3-5 minutes, until cooked and golden.
Serve, garnished with fresh herb sprigs.

Serving suggestion
Serve with lightly buttered bread or toast.

Variations
Use mussels or oysters in place of scallops. Use brown or wholemeal breadcrumbs in place of white.
Use 4-6 spring onions in place of shallots or small onions.

Salmon in Mustard Sauce

A delicious way to prepare fresh salmon, slow-marinated in fragrant coriander seeds, dill and sugar, then served with a piquant mustard sauce.

Preparation time: 20 minutes, plus 1-2 days marinating time • Serves: 8-10

Ingredients

1 kg (2 lb 4 oz) fresh salmon (middle cut)	*7.5 ml (1½ tsp) Dijon mustard*
5 coriander seeds	*30 ml (2 tbsp) white wine vinegar*
30 ml (2 tbsp) caster sugar	*75 ml (5 tbsp) olive oil*
2.5 ml (½ tsp) freshly ground black pepper	*Lettuce leaves*
5 ml (1 tsp) coarse sea salt	*2.5 ml (½ tsp) red peppercorns*
2 sprigs of fresh dill, coarsely chopped, plus 15 ml (1 tbsp) finely chopped fresh dill	*Fresh dill sprigs, to garnish*

Method

1

Slice the salmon in half lengthways, removing and discarding the bones.

2

Grind the coriander seeds and mix with 15 ml (1 tbsp) sugar, pepper and salt. Rub the mixture all over the salmon.

3

Sprinkle the coarsely chopped dill over the halves of fish.

4

Fold the halves of fish back over themselves, place in a dish and cover with cling film or place in an ovenproof dish and cover.

5

Place a board on top and weight it down with, for example, canned food, then set aside in a cool place for 1-2 days.
Turn the fish several times during this period.

6

Scrape the herbs off the fish, remove and discard the skin, then cut the flesh into thin slices.

7

For the mustard sauce, in a bowl, mix the mustard with the remaining 15 ml (1 tbsp) sugar, wine vinegar and oil, then add the finely chopped dill and mix well.

8

Arrange a few lettuce leaves on a serving platter, place the fish on top of the lettuce and cover with some of the mustard sauce.

9

Sprinkle with the peppercorns, then pour the remainder of the mustard sauce over the fish.
Serve, garnished with fresh dill sprigs.

Serving suggestion

Serve with lightly buttered thin slices of brown or wholemeal bread.

Variations

Use fresh parsley, tarragon or oregano in place of dill. Use mustard seeds in place of coriander seeds.
Use green peppercorns in place of red.

Cook's tip

Grind the coriander seeds using a pestle and mortar, or use a coffee grinder.

Mixed Seafood Flan

This is a seafood variation on the basic quiche. A pastry flan case is filled with a cheese custard
and a mixture of mussels, prawns and clams.

Preparation time: 45 minutes, plus chilling time • Cooking time: 25 minutes • Serves: 6

Ingredients

280 g (10 oz) plain flour	200 g (7 oz) small scallops
Salt and freshly ground black pepper	200 ml (7 fl oz) milk
1 medium egg yolk	300 ml (½ pint) cream
125 g (4½ oz) butter, at room temperature	4 medium eggs
1 litre (1¾ pints) mussels, in their shells	100 g (3½ oz) Gruyère cheese, grated
450 g (1 lb) cockles, in their shells	Grated nutmeg
200 ml (7 fl oz) white wine	Fresh dill sprigs, to garnish
200 g (7 oz) medium cooked whole prawns	

Method

1
For the pastry, in a bowl, mix together the flour, 50 ml (2 fl oz) water, salt and egg yolk.
Add the softened butter and mix into the dough.

2
Work the pastry dough into a ball, cover and allow to rest in the refrigerator for 30 minutes.

3
Rinse and scrub clean the mussels and cockles. Use several changes of water to eliminate all the sand and grit.

4
Place the mussels and cockles in separate saucepans, each containing half the wine.
Cover and cook for about 5 minutes, until the shells open. Drain and allow to cool.

5
Shell the prawns, then cut into small pieces. Wash the scallops and discard the corals.
Remove the mussels and cockles from their shells.

6
In a bowl, mix together the milk, cream, eggs, grated cheese, salt and pepper to taste and a few gratings of nutmeg. Set aside.

7
Roll out the pastry on a lightly floured surface using a floured rolling pin.

8
Use the pastry to line a 25-cm (10-in) flan dish. Trim off the excess pastry. Prick the base of the pastry with a fork.

9
Drain all excess fluid from the cooked seafood. Arrange with the uncooked scallops in the bottom of the pastry case.

10
Pour over the milk mixture and cook in a preheated oven at 240°C/475°F/Gas Mark 9 for 25 minutes.
Cover with a sheet of foil, if necessary, to prevent over-browning.

11
Remove from the flan case and serve warm, cut into wedges. Garnish with fresh dill sprigs.

Serving suggestions
Serve small slices as a first course or larger ones for a main dish, accompanied with a tossed green salad.

Variations
Use Emmenthal or Cheddar cheese in place of Gruyère. Use red wine in place of white wine.

Cook's tip
To save time, use a ready-cooked plain pastry case and reduce the oven temperature to 200°C/400°C/Gas Mark 6.

Marinated Raw Fish

This makes a lovely light starter to any meal. Thinly sliced salmon and ocean perch fillets are 'cooked' in a lemon juice and olive oil marinade flavoured with shallot and pepper and served with sliced vegetables.

Preparation time: 40 minutes, plus 10 minutes marinating time • Serves: 6

Ingredients

½ small salmon, weighing about 700 g (1 lb 9 oz), halved lengthways	1 curly endive
	2 sprigs of fresh dill
Ocean perch fillets, weighing about 300 g (10½ oz)	2 lemons
1 carrot	Salt
½ cucumber	Mixed peppercorns in a pepper mill
1 stick celery	60 ml (4 tbsp) olive oil
2 shallots	1 small jar lumpfish roe and fresh dill sprigs, to garnish

Method

1
Sice the salmon very thinly with a sharp, serrated knife.

2
Arrange the slices around the rim of a serving platter, overlapping them.

3
Cut smaller slices of the perch fillets in the same way as the salmon.

4
Intersperse the perch slices with the salmon, working towards the centre of the platter.

5
Peel and cut the carrot into thin slices. Cut the slices into very thin julienne (matchsticks). Set aside.

6
Cut the cucumber into chunks. Peel thickly using a sharp knife, discarding the core. Cut the peel into julienne and set aside.

7
Peel the celery, then cut into thin, even slices with a vegetable peeler. Cut into julienne and set aside.

8
Peel the shallots and halve them lengthways. Finely and evenly chop the halves.

9
Trim the endive and the dill. Discard the stalks of the dill and finely chop the leaves.

10
Squeeze the lemons and mix the juice with the shallots and dill leaves in a bowl.

11
Season the lemon juice and dill mixture with salt and a few turns of the pepper mill, then whisk in the oil.

12
Brush some sauce over all the fish. Marinate for 10 minutes, then serve with the endive and julienned vegetables tossed in the remaining sauce. Garnish with the lumpfish roe and fresh dill sprigs.

Serving suggestion
Serve with fresh bread rolls.

Variations
Use radicchio in place of endive. Use limes in place of lemons.

Cook's tip
It is essential to this recipe that the fish is exceptionally fresh.

Languoustine in Puff Pastry

These fresh Dublin Bay prawn appetisers are ideal for entertaining or for canapés at parties.

Preparation time: 20 minutes • Cooking time: 10 minutes • Makes: 36

Ingredients

600 g (1 lb 5 oz) frozen puff or flaky pastry	*500 g (1 lb 2 oz) frozen Dublin Bay prawns, thawed*
175 g (6 oz) fresh Parmesan cheese, grated	
Paprika, to taste	*12-15 closed cup or button mushrooms, sliced*
1 medium egg	*20 stuffed olives, sliced*
45 ml (3 tbsp) milk	*Fresh chervil leaves, to garnish*

Method

1

Cut the pastry into 18 squares, each about 7.5 x 7.5 cm (3 x 3 in), then cut each square diagonally in half to make 36 triangles.

2

In a bowl, mix the Parmesan cheese with the paprika and set aside.

3

In a jug, beat the egg and milk together and brush the triangles of pastry with the mixture.

4

Place 3 prawns, 1 slice mushroom and 3 slices stuffed olives on each triangle of pastry, then sprinkle with some cheese.

5

Place on a baking tray which has been rinsed with cold water.

6

Bake in a preheated oven at 200°C/400°F/Gas Mark 6 for about 10 minutes, until cooked.

7

Serve immediately, garnished with fresh chervil leaves.

Serving suggestions

Serve with a mixed leaf salad or homemade coleslaw.

Variations

Use cooked, shelled mussels in place of prawns. Use Cheddar or Gruyère cheese in place of Parmesan.

Spicy Potted Shrimps

This favourite seafood starter is given a new twist with the addition of ground spices to the butter.

Preparation time: 10 minutes, plus standing and chilling time • Cooking time: 3 minutes (microwave) • Serves: 4

Ingredients

350 g (12 oz) cooked fresh or frozen shrimps	2.5 ml (½ tsp) freshly ground black pepper
175 g (6 oz) butter	2.5 ml (½ tsp) paprika
5 ml (1 tsp) grated nutmeg	Lemon wedges and small parsley or dill sprigs, to garnish
2.5 ml (½ tsp) ground ginger	

Method

1

If using frozen shrimps, defrost and dry well on absorbent kitchen paper.

2

To clarify the butter, heat in a microwave-proof bowl in a microwave oven on MEDIUM for 2 minutes.
Leave the butter to stand for about 15 minutes.

3

Skim the salt from the top of the butter and carefully pour or spoon off the clear butter oil.
Discard the milky sediment in the bottom of the dish.

4

Combine the clarified butter and the spices in a clean microwave-proof bowl and cook for 1 minute on HIGH.

5

Stir in the shrimps and spoon the mixture into 4 ramekin dishes, pressing down firmly.

6

Cover and chill until firm.

7

To serve, turn out the potted shrimps onto small plates and garnish with lemon wedges and sprigs of parsley or dill.

Serving suggestions

Serve with melba toast or hot wholemeal toast triangles.

Variations

Use small prawns in place of shrimps. Use ground cinnamon in place of nutmeg or ginger.

Cook's tip

This dish can be prepared a day in advance and kept in the refrigerator.

Grilled Oysters

Grilled fresh oysters are topped with a herby almond mixture in this delicious dish.

Preparation time: 15 minutes • Cooking time: 5 minutes • Serves: 6

Ingredients

18 fresh oysters	*Juice of ½ lemon*
30 ml (2 tbsp) ground almonds	*15 ml (1 tbsp) Cognac*
100 g (3½ oz) soft butter	*Freshly ground black pepper*
1 clove garlic, crushed	*15 ml (1 tbsp) flaked almonds*
½ bunch of fresh parsley	

Method

1

To prepare the oysters, place a clean tea-towel on the work surface, then with an oyster knife pressed against the hinge of the shell, prise each shell apart. Set aside.

2

In a bowl, mix the ground almonds with the butter and garlic. Set aside.

3

Chop the parsley and mix with the lemon juice, Cognac, pepper and almond butter.

4

Spoon the almond mixture evenly over the oyster flesh in the shells.

5

Sprinkle with the flaked almonds and grill under a preheated grill until golden brown. Serve immediately.

Serving suggestion

Serve with thin slices of buttered bread or toast.

Variations

Use scallops in place of oysters. Use basil or chives in place of parsley. Use lime juice in place of lemon juice.

Cook's tip

Ready-prepared 'lazy' garlic is available in jars, to save a little time.

Curried Prawn Soup

A quick-to-prepare and colourful soup with the spicy taste of curry and the sharp flavour of apple.

Preparation time: 15 minutes, plus standing time • Cooking time: 8-9 minutes (microwave on HIGH) • Serves: 4

Ingredients

40 g (1½ oz) butter or margarine	40 g (1½ oz) plain flour
15 ml (1 tbsp) curry powder	600 ml (1 pint) fish or vegetable stock
1 shallot, finely chopped	600 ml (1 pint) milk
1 eating apple, peeled, quartered, cored and cut into dice	350-450 g (12 oz-1 lb) cooked, shelled prawns
	150 ml (¼ pint) plain yogurt

Method

1

Place the butter or margarine and curry powder in a microwave-proof bowl and cook in a microwave oven for 1 minute on HIGH, until melted.

2

Stir in the shallot and apple and cook for a further 2 minutes on HIGH.

3

Stir in the flour and when well blended, pour on the stock. Stir well, then cook for a further 4 minutes on HIGH, or until thickened, stirring once or twice.

4

Remove from the oven and leave to cool. Pour into a food processor or blender and purée until smooth, then pour into a microwave-proof bowl.

5

Add the milk, stir to mix, then cook for 1-2 minutes on HIGH.

6

Stir in the prawns and leave to stand for 2-3 minutes before serving. Top with yogurt and serve.

Serving suggestion
Serve with crusty bread rolls.

Variations
25 g (1 oz) cooked rice can be added to each serving. Heat through thoroughly before adding the prawns. Use shrimps or mussels in place of prawns. Use 1 pear in place of the apple. Use 5-10 ml (1-2 tsp) chilli powder in place of curry powder.

Cook's tip
Cooking curry powder, or other spices, before adding liquid gives it a more mellow flavour.

Spanish Fish Stew

A delicious stew of mixed fish, seafood and vegetables.

Preparation time: 15 minutes • Cooking time: about 23 minutes (microwave) • Serves: 6

Ingredients

1 onion, thinly sliced	*5 black peppercorns*
1 clove garlic, thinly sliced	*2 whole cloves*
45 ml (3 tbsp) olive oil	*A pinch of saffron*
250 g (9 oz) leeks, sliced in half lengthways	*750 g (1 lb 10 oz) filleted white fish, such as cod or bass*
1 small bulb fennel, sliced into strips	*200 g (7 oz) cooked mussels*
1.4 litres (2½ pints) fish stock	*100 g (3½ oz) fresh, cooked crab meat*
1 bay leaf	*175 g (6 oz) cooked, shelled prawns*

Method

1

Place the onion and garlic in a large microwave-proof dish with the oil, cover and cook
in a microwave oven for 3 minutes on HIGH.

2

Add the leeks and fennel to the onion and garlic, stir to mix and cook in the microwave for 3 minutes on HIGH.

3

Add the stock, bay leaf, peppercorns, cloves and saffron and stir to mix.

4

Cook for a further 9 minutes on HIGH.

5

Meanwhile, cut the fillets of fish into small pieces about 3-cm (1¼-in) square.

6

Add the fish to the stock mixture, cover and cook in the microwave for 3 minutes on HIGH.

7

Stir, then cook for a further 2 minutes on MEDIUM.

8

Add the mussels, crab meat and prawns to the dish and stir to mix. Cover and cook for 3 minutes on HIGH.

9

Remove and discard the bay leaf, peppercorns and cloves and ladle the stew into warmed bowls to serve.

Serving suggestion

Serve with thick slices of fresh crusty bread or toast.

Variations

Use 4-6 shallots in place of onion. Use smoked fish such as cod or haddock in place of white fish.
Use cooked scallops in place of mussels.

Cream of Sweetcorn Soup with Smoked Salmon

A wonderfully creamy and flavourful soup made extra quick and easy by cooking in the microwave.

Preparation time: 10 minutes • Cooking time: about 10 minutes (microwave on HIGH) • Serves: 2-4

Ingredients

15 ml (1 tbsp) cornflour	*75 g (2³⁄₄ oz) herb-flavoured crème fraîche*
850 ml (1½ pints) chicken stock	*15 ml (1 tbsp) fresh chopped dill*
1 medium egg	*75 g (2³⁄₄ oz) smoked salmon, finely chopped or sliced*
140 g (5 oz) canned sweetcorn kernels	*Freshly ground black pepper*

Method

1

Blend the cornflour with the stock in a microwave-proof dish.

2

Separate the egg yolk and white and stir the yolk into the stock mixture. Set aside the egg white.

3

Cover the dish and cook in a microwave oven for 7-8 minutes on HIGH, stirring once.

4

Add the sweetcorn to the stock with the crème fraîche and stir to mix. Cover and cook for a further 3 minutes on HIGH.

5

Lightly beat the egg white until slightly stiff and fold into the soup.

6

Add the dill, smoked salmon and pepper to taste to the soup and stir to mix.

7

Ladle into warmed soup bowls and serve immediately.

Serving suggestion

Serve with fresh bread rolls or crusty French bread.

Variations

Use fresh parsley or tarragon in place of dill. Use smoked trout in place of smoked salmon.

Cook's tip

To make your own herb-flavoured crème fraîche, simply fold chopped fresh herbs into a pot of crème fraîche. Choose your favourite herb mixture.

Shrimp Soup

The adition of fresh mixed vegetables to this shrimp soup creates a filling and tasty supper dish.

Preparation time: 15 minutes • Cooking time: 25 minutes • Serves: 4

Ingredients

50 g (1¾ oz) butter	250 ml (9 fl oz) white wine
½ celeriac, diced	30 ml (2 tbsp) flour
1 onion, finely chopped	2 medium egg yolks
2 baby carrots, cut into thin strips	250 g (9 oz) cooked, shelled shrimps
1 leek, cut into thin strips	Salt and freshly ground black pepper
850 ml (1½ pints) fish or vegetable stock	Fresh herb sprigs, to garnish

Method

1

Heat the butter in a pan, add the vegetables and cook for 5 minutes, stirring occasionally.

2

Add the stock, cover and cook for about 15 minutes, stirring occasionally.

3

Add the wine. Mix the flour with a little cold water, then stir into the soup. Bring to the boil, stirring. Simmer for 3 minutes, stirring.

4

Mix the egg yolks in a cup with a little stock, then stir into the soup.

5

Add the shrimps and allow to warm through, stirring. Season to taste with salt and pepper.

6

Spoon into soup bowls and serve, garnished with fresh herb sprigs.

Serving suggestion
Serve with sesame bread or mixed seed bread.

Variations
Use small prawns in place of shrimps. Use small parsnips in place of carrots. Use swede in place of celeriac.

Cold Mussel Soup with Saffron

This is an elegant seafood soup – ideal for warm summer evenings. The flavour of saffron perfectly complements the mussels.

Preparation time: 45 minutes, plus chilling time • Cooking time: 10 minutes • Serves: 6

Ingredients

1 litre (1¾ pints) fresh mussels	A pinch of saffron powder
2 shallots, finely chopped	6 slices French bread
Salt and freshly ground black pepper	1 clove garlic
300 ml (½ pint) white wine	1 jar lumpfish roe
½ cucumber	30 ml (2 tbsp) fresh chives, chopped
600 ml (1 pint) fish stock	Saffron fronds
300 ml (½ pint) double cream	Fresh dill sprigs, to garnish

Method

1

Scrape and remove the beards from the mussels. Soak and wash thoroughly.

2

Place the mussels in a large frying pan, add the shallots, pepper to taste and white wine and cook, covered, for 7 minutes. Remove the mussels from the heat and set aside to cool. Remove from the shells and set aside.

3

Strain the cooking juices through a sieve lined with a piece of muslin and reserve the liquid.

4

Peel the cucumber lengthways with a vegetable peeler, then cut the cucumber into chunks. Remove bands of flesh, working down to the centre and seeds. Cut the flesh into a fine julienne (matchsticks) and set aside.

5

In a casserole dish, bring the stock, mussel cooking liquid, cream and saffron powder to the boil.

6

Season with salt and pepper, remove from the heat and allow to cool. Refrigerate for 2 hours.

7

Toast the slices of bread evenly on each side.

8

Remove and discard the central shoot from the garlic. Rub the garlic over the toasts and spoon some lumpfish roe over each slice. Sprinkle with chives.

9

Arrange the mussels, cucumber and toasts in bowls and pour over the chilled stock. Sprinkle the saffron fronds over the soup just before serving, and garnish with fresh dill sprigs.

Serving suggestion

Serve with warm ciabatta or country-style bread.

Variations

Use fresh scallops in place of mussels. Use ciabatta in place of French bread. Use chopped parsley or tarragon in place of chives.

Cheese and Clam Chowder

Chowders are quick, creamy soups which are as filling as a main course. This tasty example
is enriched with Red Leicester cheese.

Preparation time: 15 minutes • Cooking time: 25 minutes • Serves: 4

Ingredients

25 g (1 oz) butter or margarine	350 g (12 oz) potatoes, diced
1 onion, finely chopped	1.25 ml (¼ tsp) dried thyme
2 sticks celery, chopped	Salt and freshly ground black pepper
1 green pepper, chopped	1 bay leaf
25 g (1 oz) plain flour	115 g (4 oz) Red Leicester cheese, grated
2.5 ml (½ tsp) dry mustard	A dash of Worcestershire sauce
1 litre (1¾ pints) milk	Single cream (optional)
900 g (2 lb) canned clams, liquid reserved	30 ml (2 tbsp) chopped fresh parsley

Method

1
Melt the butter or margarine in a heavy-based saucepan, add the onion, celery and pepper
and cook for about 5 minutes, until softened, stirring occasionally.

2
Mix in the flour and mustard and cook for 3 minutes, stirring continuously.

3
Add the milk and clam liquid and continue to stir until the mixture comes to the boil and thickens.

4
Add the potatoes, thyme, salt and pepper and bay leaf and stir to mix. Cover and simmer for about 12 minutes,
until the potatoes are just tender.

5
Remove and discard the bay leaf and stir in the clams. Cover and simmer for a further 3-4 minutes.

6
Add the cheese and Worcestershire sauce, stir to mix and cook until the cheese has melted.

7
Add single cream to thin the soup if it is too thick. Garnish with the parsley and serve immediately.

Serving suggestion
Serve with thick slices of fresh bread or bread rolls.

Variations
Use canned mussels or cockles in place of clams. Use sweet potatoes in place of standard potatoes.
Use fresh basil in place of parsley.

Mussels with Rice

A hearty stew of mussels, rice and vegetables with a touch of sweetness provided by sultanas.

Preparation time: 10 minutes • Cooking time: 35 minutes • Serves: 4-6

Ingredients

About 800 g (1 lb 12 oz) cooked mussels, cooking liquid reserved	*1 onion, finely chopped*
50 g (1¾ oz) butter	*500 g (1 lb 2 oz) tomatoes, skinned and roughly chopped*
250 g (9 oz) rice	*250 ml (9 fl oz) dry white wine*
50 g (1¾ oz) sultanas	*Salt and freshly ground black pepper*
60 ml (4 tbsp) olive oil	*Sprigs of fresh chervil, to garnish*

Method

1

Drain the mussels thoroughly, retaining the cooking liquid, and set aside.

2

Melt the butter in a flameproof casserole dish and cook the rice and sultanas until
the rice becomes transparent, stirring continuously.

3

Add about 500 ml (18 fl oz) water, cover and cook for about 15 minutes over a gentle heat,
until the rice is cooked and tender. Drain.

4

Meanwhile, heat the oil in a pan and cook the onion until softened, stirring occasioally.
Add the tomatoes and wine and bring to the boil.

5

Add the mussels to the pan and stir to warm through.

6

Stir in the cooked rice and sultanas with some of the mussel cooking liquid. Season to taste with salt and pepper.

7

Transfer the mixture to an ovenproof dish and bake in a preheated oven at 200°C/400°F/Gas Mark 6 for 10 minutes.
Serve, garnished with fresh chervil sprigs.

Serving suggestion

Serve with mixed seed bread or soda bread.

Variations

Use chopped ready-to-eat dried apricots in place of sultanas. Use a 400-g (14-oz) can chopped tomatoes
in place of fresh tomatoes.

Prawns in Melon

Deliciously cool and refreshing for a summer lunch, this recipe could also be served
as an unusual starter for 8 people.

Preparation time: 25 minutes, plus chilling time • Serves: 4

Ingredients

2 small melons	*30 ml (2 tbsp) chopped fresh mint,*
4 medium tomatoes	*plus 4 sprigs for garnish*
1 small cucumber	*A pinch of sugar*
1 orange	*Salt and freshly ground black pepper*
Juice of ½ lemon	*5 ml (1 tsp) chopped fresh lemon thyme (optional)*
60 ml (4 tbsp) sunflower oil	*225 g (8 oz) shelled prawns*
45 ml (3 tbsp) double cream	*85 g (3 oz) toasted flaked almonds, to garnish*

Method

1

Cut the melons in half through the middle, remove the seeds and scoop out the flesh with a melon baller or spoon.
Leave a 5-mm (¼-in) border of fruit on the inside of each shell and reserve.

2

Cut the melon flesh into 1-cm (½-in) cubes or leave in balls. Skin the tomatoes and remove and discard the seeds.
Cut the flesh into strips.

3

Peel the cucumber and cut in half lengthways, then into 1-cm (½-in) cubes. Peel and segment the orange.

4

In a bowl, mix together the lemon juice, oil and cream.

5

Stir in the mint, sugar, salt and pepper to taste and lemon thyme, if using.

6

Add the prawns and the prepared fruit and vegetables, and mix thoroughly to coat evenly with the dressing.

7

Pile equal quantities of the fruit and prawn mixture into the 4 melon shells and chill thoroughly.

8

Serve, garnished with the reserved mint sprigs and the flaked almonds.

Servings suggestion
Serve with a mixed green salad and new potatoes.

Variations
Use 1 pink grapefruit in place of the orange. Use basil or parsley in place of mint.

Cook's tip
If the melon shells will not stand upright, cut a thin slice off the bottom of each one to make them more stable.

Salade Niçoise

This classic French salad featuring tuna, prawns and anchovies is a meal in itself when served on a bed of crisp mixed lettuce leaves with some crusty bread.

Preparation time: 20 minutes • Serves: 4

Ingredients

2 large or 6 small new potatoes, cooked and cut into 1-cm (¹/₂-in) dice	*4 hard-boiled eggs, shelled and quartered lengthways*
175 g (6 oz) French beans, trimmed and cooked	*60-g (2¹/₄-oz) can anchovies, drained and chopped*
85 g (3 oz) black olives, halved and stoned	*90 ml (6 tbsp) olive oil*
1 small cucumber, diced	*30 ml (2 tbsp) white wine vinegar*
4 tomatoes, cut into 8 segments	*45 ml (3 tbsp) chopped fresh mixed herbs*
200-g (7-oz) can tuna in brine	*10 ml (2 tsp) French mustard*
115 g (4 oz) shelled prawns	*Salt and freshly ground black pepper*

Method

1

In a large bowl, mix together the potatoes, beans, olives, cucumber and tomatoes.

2

Drain the tuna and flake with a fork. Mix with the potato mixture along with the prawns, eggs and anchovies.

3

In a small bowl, whisk together the oil, wine vinegar, herbs and mustard. Whisk until thick.

4

Pour the dressing over the salad ingredients and stir gently to coat evenly. Season to taste and serve.

Serving suggestion
Serve with crusty French bread.

Variations
Use canned salmon in place of tuna. Use mangetout in place of French beans. Use cooked, shelled mussels in place of prawns.

Cook's tip
If you have a screw-top jar, the dressing ingredients can be placed in this and shaken vigorously until they have thickened. The dressing will keep up to 2 weeks in a refrigerator, so make double the quantity and use the extra to enliven another salad meal.

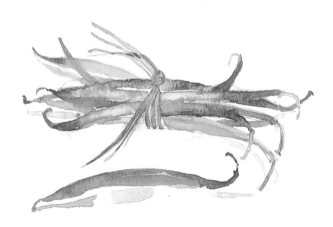

Crab Salad in Orange Shells

This crab salad is attractively served in hollowed-out orange shells. The addition of the orange flesh gives a contrasting sweet and acid taste to the seafood and vegetables.

Preparation time: 35 minutes • Serves: 6

Ingredients

3 or 6 small oranges	5 ml (1 tsp) Cognac
1 avocado pear	A few drops of Tabasco sauce
Juice of 1 lemon	5 ml (1 tsp) Worcestershire sauce
1 egg yolk	1/2 onion
5 ml (1 tsp) mustard	100 g (3 1/2 oz) small prawns
Salt and freshly ground black pepper	10 crab sticks, weighing about 300 g (10 1/2 oz) in total
200 ml (7 fl oz) vegetable oil	2 tomatoes
15 ml (1 tbsp) tomato ketchup	Fresh chervil sprigs, to garnish

Method

1
Halve the oranges and remove the flesh without crushing. Reserve the shells for presentation. Cube the orange flesh and set aside.

2
Halve the avocado, remove and discard the stone, then peel the fruit. Dice the flesh and place in a bowl. Coat with lemon juice to prevent discoloration.

3
In a bowl, mix together the egg yolk, mustard and salt and pepper to taste. Gradually whisk in the oil to make a mayonnaise.

4
When thick, add the ketchup, Cognac, Tabasco and Worcestershire sauce. Mix thoroughly.

5
Halve the onion and finely chop. Set aside. Shell the prawns and set aside.

6
Cut the crab sticks in half, then shred. Set aside.

7
Remove the stalks from the tomatoes. Plunge into a bowl of boiling water for 10 seconds, then plunge the tomatoes into cold water. Peel off the skin and cube the flesh, discarding the juice and seeds. Reserve 30 ml (2 tbsp) for decoration.

8
Mix all the prepared ingredients into the mayonnaise and adjust the seasoning.

9
Fill each orange shell with the mixed salad and garnish with the reserved tomato and chervil sprigs. Serve.

Serving suggestion
Serve with minted boiled new potatoes and a crisp mixed salad.

Variations
Use pink grapefruit in place of oranges. Use 1 mango in place of the avocado. Use fresh or canned crab meat in place of prawns.

King Prawn Salad

A mouthwatering sauce complements the sautéed prawns in this delicious salad.

Preparation time: 25 minutes • Cooking time: 30 minutes • Serves: 4

Ingredients

20 fresh king prawns	15 ml (1 tbsp) double cream
30 ml (2 tbsp) olive oil	55 g (2 oz) butter
1 carrot, finely sliced	5 ml (1 tsp) wine vinegar
½ onion, finely sliced	Salt and freshly ground black pepper
15 ml (1 tbsp) crushed tomato pulp	4 small servings of mixed salad leaves
½ bay leaf	Fresh herb sprigs, to garnish
5 ml (1 tsp) Cognac	

Method

1
Shell and devein the prawns and set aside, discarding the heads but retaining the shells for the sauce.

2
To make the sauce, heat 15 ml (1 tbsp) oil in a pan and fry the carrot, onion, tomato pulp, prawn shells and bay leaf for 2 minutes, stirring occasionally. Drain away the excess fat.

3
Deglaze the pan with the Cognac and pour water over to cover the ingredients.

4
Continue cooking, reducing the liquid until it is quite thick, stirring occasionally.

5
Strain the sauce through a very fine sieve into a jug, pressing the prawn shells to extract the juice. Keep warm.

6
Melt the butter in a frying pan and cook the prawns for 2 minutes, stirring.

7
Stir the wine vinegar into the prawn sauce. Season with salt and pepper, then whisk in the remaining oil.

8
Serve the prawns on a bed of salad leaves with the sauce spooned over. Garnish with fresh herb sprigs.

Serving suggestion
Add diced tomato and a little finely diced green pepper to the salad if you like. Serve with baked potatoes.

Variations
Use 1 parsnip in place of the carrot. Use 1 leek in place of the onion. Use passata in place of tomato pulp.

Cook's tip
When reducing the prawn sauce, reduce to about 75 ml (2½ fl oz), then add the wine vinegar a little at a time, as well as the oil, and season to taste.

Prawn and Cashew Nuts in Pineapple

Served in pineapple shells, this impressive salad is ideal for a special summer lunch or buffet.

Preparation time: 30 minutes • Cooking time: 10-15 minutes • Serves: 4

Ingredients

2 small fresh pineapples, with nice green tops	*1 medium egg*
225 g (8 oz) cooked, shelled prawns	*30 ml (2 tbsp) caster sugar*
115 g (4 oz) roasted, unsalted cashew nuts	*15 ml (1 tbsp) tarragon vinegar*
2 sticks celery, thinly sliced	*10 ml (2 tsp) chopped fresh tarragon*
60 ml (4 tbsp) lemon juice	*125 ml (4 fl oz) whipping cream*

Method

1

Cut the pineapples carefully in half lengthways, leaving their green tops attached.

2

Cut out the pineapple flesh carefully, leaving a 5-mm (¼-in) border of flesh on the inside of the shells. Remove and discard the cores and cut the flesh into bite-sized pieces.

3

Place the chopped pineapple into a bowl, along with the prawns, cashew nuts and celery. Add the lemon juice and mix well. Divide the mixture equally between the pineapple shells and chill in the refrigerator.

4

In a heatproof bowl, whisk together the egg and sugar. Stand the bowl over a pan of simmering water, then whisk in the vinegar and tarragon. Continue whisking until the mixture has thickened.

5

Remove the bowl from the heat and allow to cool completely, whisking occasionally.

6

When completely cold, whip the cream until it is just beginning to thicken, then fold into the dressing mixture.

7

Pour the cream dressing over the salad in the pineapple shells and serve.

Serving suggestions

Serve with fresh bread or baked potatoes and a green salad.

Variations

Use mangoes in place of pineapple. Use almonds or hazelnuts in place of cashew nuts.
Use cooked, shelled mussels or cockles in place of prawns.

Cook's tips

Whisking the egg and sugar dressing can be done with an electric whisk. It will not then be necessary to whisk the dressing over a pan of hot water. If you cannot buy unsalted cashew nuts, wash salted ones in water, but make sure they are completely dry before adding to the salad.

Spanish Rice and Sole Salad

A substantial salad which is ideal for a summer lunch.

Preparation time: 20 minutes • Cooking time: 15-20 minutes • Serves: 4

Ingredients

2 large lemon sole, each filleted into 4 pieces	1 green pepper, seeded and chopped into 5-mm (¼-in) dice
4-6 black peppercorns	15 ml (1 tbsp) chopped fresh mixed herbs
A slice of onion	45 ml (3 tbsp) French dressing
15 ml (1 tbsp) lemon juice	300 ml (½ pint) mayonnaise
Salt and freshly ground black pepper	1 clove garlic, crushed
175 g (6 oz) long-grain rice	5 ml (1 tsp) tomato purée
1 small aubergine	5 ml (1 tsp) paprika
30 ml (2 tbsp) olive oil	Watercress sprigs, to garnish
1 shallot, finely chopped	

Method

1

Lay the sole fillets in an ovenproof dish together with the peppercorns, onion, lemon juice and just enough water to cover. Sprinkle with a little salt and cover the dish with foil or a lid. Poach in a preheated oven at 180°C/350°F/Gas Mark 4 for 8-10 minutes. Allow the fish to cool in the liquor, then cut each fillet into 2.5-cm (1-in) pieces. Discard the liquor, peppercorns and onion.

2

Cook the rice in a pan of boiling water for about 10-15 minutes, until soft. Rinse in cold water, drain, then separate the grains with a fork.

3

Cut the aubergine in half and sprinkle with 10 ml (2 tsp) salt. Allow to stand for 30 minutes, then rinse very thoroughly. Pat dry and cut into 1-cm (½-in) dice.

4

Heat the oil in a large frying pan and fry the aubergine until soft.

5

Remove from the heat and allow the aubergine to cool, then mix into the rice in a bowl along with the shallot, pepper, half the chopped herbs and the French dressing.

6

In a bowl, mix together the mayonnaise, garlic, tomato purée, paprika, remaining herbs and seasoning.

7

Arrange the rice mixture on one side of a serving dish and the cooked sole pieces on the other.
Spoon the mayonnaise over the sole and garnish the dish with watercress. Serve.

Serving suggestions
Serve with crusty French bread or oatcakes or crackers.

Variations
Use plaice in place of lemon sole. Use 2-3 spring onions in place of the shallot. Use 1 large courgette in place of the aubergine.

Cook's tips
Cooked rice weighs about twice its dry weight. Rice can be cooked and frozen in convenient amounts. To use, the frozen rice should be placed straight into boiling water and allowed to cook for 3-4 minutes, then rinsed in cold water.

Pan-Braised Fish

A sumptuous dish of mixed fish and vegetables flavoured with garlic and fresh herbs.

Preparation time: 15 minutes • Cooking time: 35 minutes • Serves: 4

Ingredients

250 g (9 oz) cod fillet	1 bulb fennel, cut into 8 segments
250 g (9 oz) bass fillet	4 large tomatoes, skinned and chopped
500 g (1 lb 2 oz) cleaned and gutted eel	1 bay leaf
90 ml (6 tbsp) white wine vinegar	1 sprig of fresh thyme
75 ml (5 tbsp) olive oil	Salt and freshly ground black pepper
2 large onions, finely chopped	25 g (1 oz) fresh parsley, finely chopped
2 cloves garlic, crushed	

Method

1

Place the fish and eel in a shallow dish and sprinkle with wine vinegar. Set aside.

2

Heat the oil in a pan, add the onion, garlic, fennel and tomatoes and cook for about 15 minutes, stirring occasionally.

3

Add the bay leaf and thyme to the pan, then slice the fish into small pieces and lay over the vegetables.

4

Season to taste with salt and pepper, then simmer for about 20 minutes, stirring occasionally and gently.
Discard the bay leaf and thyme.

5

Sprinkle the parsley over the fish and serve.

Serving suggestions

Serve with fresh crusty French bread or croquette potatoes.

Variations

Us 4 leeks in place of onions. Use fresh tuna or salmon in place of eel. Use chives or tarragon in place of parsley.

Fried Fish in Batter

Battered mixed fish simply deep-fried is always a popular choice with family and friends for a tasty supper.

Preparation time: 20 minutes, plus 30 minutes standing time • Cooking time: 10 minutes • Serves: 4

Ingredients

750 g (1 lb 10 oz) mixed fish, such as cod and salmon fillets	*1 medium egg*
Lemon juice	*125 ml (4 fl oz) milk*
Salt	*15 ml (1 tbsp) melted butter or oil*
100 g (3½ oz) plain flour	*Hot oil, for deep-frying*
	Fresh herb sprigs, to garnish

Method

1

Place the fish in a bowl and sprinkle with lemon juice. Leave to stand for 30 minutes.

2

Pat the fish dry with absorbent kitchen paper, season with salt, then cut into small pieces. Set aside.

3

For the batter, sift the flour into a bowl, then make a well in the centre.

4

Beat the egg and milk together in a bowl. Pour a little of the egg mixture into the well and beat the flour and liquid together.

5

Gradually beat in the rest of the egg mixture, then add the 15 ml (1 tbsp) butter or oil, beating well to make a smooth batter.

6

Dip each piece of fish on a fork into the batter, covering it completely. Deep-fry the battered fish in hot oil until the batter is golden brown. Drain on absorbent kitchen paper before serving. Serve, garnished with fresh herb sprigs.

Serving suggestion

Serve with oven chips, peas and carrots.

Variations

Use lime or orange juice in place of lemon juice. Use buckwheat or wholemeal flour in place of white flour.

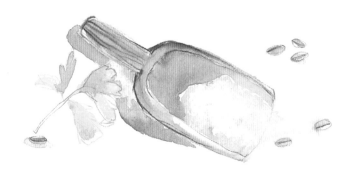

Mackerel in Creamy Pink Pepper Sauce

Mackerel is served with a creamy yet piquant sauce in this unusual fish dish.

Preparation time: 10 minutes • Cooking time: 20 minutes • Serves: 4

Ingredients

8 mackerel fillets, each weighing about 100 g (3½ oz)	50 g (1¾ oz) butter
Lemon juice	1 small onion, finely chopped
Salt	100 ml (3½ oz) dry rosé wine
5 ml (1 tsp) pink peppercorns, ground	100 ml (3½ oz) double cream
90-120 ml (6-8 tbsp) olive oil	Fresh herb sprigs, to garnish

Method

1

Slash the skin of the mackerel in several places with a sharp knife. Sprinkle the fillets with lemon juice.
Season with salt to taste and the ground pink pepper.

2

Heat the oil in a pan, add the mackerel and cook for 5 minutes on each size, until crispy and browned on the outside.

3

Remove the mackerel from the pan, place on a plate and pour away any oil. Keep warm.

4

Melt the butter in the pan, add the onion and cook until softened, stirring occasionally.

5

Add the wine, then stir in the cream and boil rapidly to reduce.

6

Season to taste with salt and pepper.

7

Serve the fried mackerel with the pepper sauce spooned over. Garnish with fresh herb sprigs.

Serving suggestion
Serve with boiled new potatoes, broccoli and carrots.

Variations
Use trout in place of mackerel. Use white wine in place of rosé. Use 2-3 shallots in place of onion.

Langoustine Tails in a Wine Sauce

Langoustine tails are lightly cooked in a wine and parsley flavoured sauce to create this appetising dish.

Preparation time: 15 minutes • Cooking time: 8-10 minutes • Serves: 2-4

Ingredients

75 g (2¾ oz) butter	2.5 ml (½ tsp) dried oregano
2 small onions, finely chopped	Salt and freshly ground black pepper
½ clove garlic, crushed	500 g (1 lb 2 oz) uncooked, shelled langoustine tails or large prawns
4 tomatoes, skinned and thinly sliced	
250 ml (9 fl oz) dry white wine	Fresh herb sprigs, to garnish
30 ml (2 tbsp) finely chopped fresh parsley	

Method

1

Melt the butter in a flameproof casserole dish, add the onions and garlic and cook until softened, stirring occasionally.

2

Add the tomatoes to the pan and cook for 2 minutes, then add the wine and herbs. Season with salt and pepper and stir to mix.

3

Add the langoustine tails or prawns to the sauce and cook gently until cooked through, stirring occasionally.
Serve, garnished with fresh herb sprigs.

Serving suggestion

Serve with boiled rice and a chopped mixed side salad.

Variations

Use 2 leeks in place of the onions. Use red wine in place of white wine. Use fresh grated ginger in place of garlic.

Fish Curry

This fruity fish curry is quick and easy to prepare in the microwave – ideal for a mid-week supper dish.

Preparation time: 15 minutes, plus 30 minutes standing time • Cooking time: 16 minutes (microwave) • Serves: 2

Ingredients

400 g (14 oz) fish cutlets or fillets, such as bass, cod or haddock	*1 onion, finely chopped*
	25 g (1 oz) butter
Juice of 1 lemon	*250 g (9 oz) canned peas and baby carrots, drained*
Salt	*2 small bananas, sliced*
5-10 ml (1-2 tsp) curry powder	*Chopped fresh parsley*
A pinch of paprika	*Fresh herb sprigs, to garnish*

Method

1

Cut the fish into small pieces, place in a dish and sprinkle with lemon juice, salt to taste and curry powder.

2

Add the paprika, stir to mix, then leave to stand for 30 minutes.

3

Place the onion in a microwave-proof dish with the butter and cook in a microwave oven for 3 minutes on LOW.

4

Add the fish, stir to mix, then cover and cook for a further 8 minutes on LOW, stirring once or twice.

5

Add the peas and carrots and bananas to the dish. Cook in the microwave for a further 5 minutes on LOW.

6

Sprinkle with chopped parsley and serve, garnished with fresh herb sprigs.

Serving suggestion

Serve with boiled rice and fresh vegetables such as sweetcorn and cauliflower.

Variations

Use lime juice in place of lemon juice. Use chilli powder in place of curry powder.

Barbecued Fish

Whole fresh fish are delicious when cooked over charcoal coals – the perfect answer to summertime dining alfresco.

Preparation time: 15 minutes • Cooking time: 10-15 minutes • Serves: 4

Ingredients

8 whole trout or bass, cleaned and gutted	*2.5 ml (¹/₂ tsp) salt*
40 g (1¹/₂ oz) soft butter	*Freshly ground black pepper*
5 ml (1 tsp) white vermouth	*Fresh herb sprigs, to garnish*

Method

1
Wash and dry the fish on absorbent kitchen paper.

2
In a bowl, mix the butter with the vermouth, salt and pepper to taste.

3
Rub the mixture into the insides of the fish, then thread wooden kebab skewers through
the mouths of the fish and out by the tails.

4
Place the fish on a rack over hot charcoal coals and cook for 10-15 minutes, turning occasionally,
until cooked through and tender.

5
Serve, garnished with fresh herb sprigs. Remove the skewers before serving.

Serving suggestion
Serve with oven or barbecue-baked potatoes and crunchy coleslaw.

Variations
Use mackerel in place of trout or bass. Add a little chilli or curry powder to the butter mixture if you like.
Use port in place of vermouth.

Spaghetti with Crab and Bacon

In this special recipe, homemade parsley flavoured pasta is served with a creamy seafood and bacon sauce.

Preparation time: 1 hour • Cooking time: 20 minutes • Serves: 6

Ingredients

1 bunch of fresh parsley (about 90 ml/6 tbsp)	*10 crab sticks, weighing about 300 g (10½ oz) in total*
500 g (1 lb 2 oz) strong plain flour	*300 ml (½ pint) double cream*
Salt and freshly ground black pepper	*225 g (8 oz) cooked bacon, cut into pieces*
4 medium eggs	*40 g (1½ oz) butter*
15 ml (1 tsp) olive oil	*Chopped fresh chervil, to garnish*

Method

1
Trim the leaves from the parsley sprigs. Cook for 10 minutes in a pan of boiling water.
Press through a fine sieve and reserve the cooking liquid.

2
Purée the parsley with 45 ml (3 tbsp) of the cooking liquid in a food processor or blender until smooth.

3
In a bowl, mix together the flour, a little salt, eggs and 22 ml (1½ tbsp) parsley purée. Form into a ball.

4
Quarter the dough and form each piece into balls. Press each ball flat and run through a pasta machine.

5
Thin the dough progressively by passing it through the machine several times.
Flour the dough frequently throughout the operation.

6
Run the flattened strips of dough through the spaghetti cutter. Set aside.

7
Add the oil to a pan of boiling salted water and cook the spaghetti for 5 minutes. Strain and rinse, then set aside.

8
Shred the crab sticks with your fingers and set aside.

9
Heat the cream gently in a pan with the crab and bacon pieces until hot.

10
Meanwhile, heat the butter in a pan and when it bubbles, add the spaghetti – first reheated by plunging
for 30 seconds in boiling water. Mix well and season with salt and pepper

11
Place the buttered spaghetti around the edges of the dinner plates and arrange the crab and bacon sauce in the centre.
Garnish with chopped fresh chervil and serve immediately.

Serving suggestion
Serve with fresh crusty bread and a mixed leaf salad.

Variations
Use fresh or canned flaked crab, tuna or salmon in place of crab sticks. Use basil or chervil in place of parsley.

Cook's tip
To save time, use dried spaghetti instead of making your own pasta and cook in boiling salted water for 10-12 minutes.

Fillet of Plaice with Shrimps

In this tempting dish, plaice fillets are lightly pan-fried and topped with croutons and shrimps.

Preparation time: 15 minutes • Cooking time: 20-25 minutes • Serves: 6

Ingredients

18 plaice fillets, each weighing about 55 g (2 oz)	*150 g (5½ oz) butter*
Salt and freshly ground black pepper	*1 sprig of fresh parsley, chopped*
45 ml (3 tbsp) plain flour	*200 g (7 oz) cooked, shelled shrimps*
125 ml (4 fl oz) olive oil	*Fresh herb sprigs, to garnish*
4 slices toast	

Method

1

Season the fish fillets with salt and pepper, and dust each piece with flour.

2

Heat the oil in a non-stick pan, add the fish and cook gently for 10-15 minutes, until cooked and tender, turning once. Keep warm.

3

Meanwhile, cut the toast into small pieces.

4

Heat the butter in a second pan and fry the pieces of bread until golden, turning occasionally.

5

Stir in the parsley and shrimps, then season to taste with salt and pepper. Cook gently for a few minutes, until piping hot, stirring occasionally.

6

Place the fish fillets on serving plates and spoon the shrimps and croutons over the top.

7

Serve immediately, garnished with fresh herb sprigs.

Serving suggestion

Serve with boiled, minted new potatoes, green beans and braised celery.

Variations

Use sole in place of plaice. Use fresh dill in place of parsley. Use small prawns in place of shrimps.

Trout with Almonds

An unusual twist on this classic recipe – whole trout are stuffed with ham and served with a flavourful ham and almond sauce.

Preparation time: 15 minutes, plus 10 minutes standing time • Cooking time: 30 minutes • Serves: 4

Ingredients

4 whole trout, cleaned and gutted	*100-g (3½-oz) piece raw ham*
Salt and freshly ground black pepper	*2 cloves garlic, finely chopped*
Juice of 1 lemon	*1 sprig of fresh parsley, finely chopped*
15 ml (1 tbsp) vegetable oil	*60 ml (4 tbsp) flaked almonds*
4 thin slices air-cured ham	*Sherry, to taste*
Plain flour, for dusting	*Fresh parsley sprigs, to garnish*
Olive oil, for frying	

Method

1
Season the trout with salt and pepper and sprinkle with lemon juice. Place in a dish and leave in the refrigerator for 10 minutes.

2
Meanwhile, heat the vegetable oil in a pan and fry the slices of air-cured ham until cooked.

3
Stuff the trout with the cooked ham and turn the trout over in the flour.

4
Heat the olive oil in a pan and fry the trout, turning occasionally, until golden brown on both sides.

5
Remove from the pan and place in a greased ovenproof dish.

6
Cut the raw ham into cubes and fry in the oil remaining in the pan, until cooked and lightly browned.

7
Add the garlic to the pan and briefly fry with the ham.

8
Add the parsley to the pan with the almonds and allow to cook for 1-2 minutes.

9
Add a little sherry to the pan, then spoon the mixture over the trout.

10
Cook in a preheated oven at 220°C/425°F/Gas Mark 7 for 10 minutes. Serve immediately, garnished with fresh parsley sprigs.

Serving suggestion
Serve with oven-baked potatoes, broccoli and cauliflower florets.

Variations
Use mackerel in place of trout. Use lime or orange juice in place of lemon juice. Use smoked ham in place of unsmoked ham.

Lasagne with Seafood

Homemade lasagne pasta is layered with mussels, cockles and prawns in an aromatic tomato sauce, topped with grated Swiss cheese.

Preparation time: 1 hour 30 minutes, plus drying time • Cooking time: 35 minutes • Serves: 6

Ingredients

400 g (14 oz) strong plain flour	2 shallots, chopped
Salt and freshly ground black pepper	1 onion, finely chopped
4 medium eggs	2 cloves garlic, chopped
60 ml (4 tbsp) olive oil	6 tomatoes, skinned, seeded and crushed
400 g (14 oz) cockles, in their shells	30 ml (2 tbsp) chopped fresh parsley
1 litre (1¾ pints) mussels, in their shells	40 g (1½ oz) butter, melted
300 g (10½ oz) prawns	100 g (3½ oz) Gruyère cheese, grated
200 ml (7 fl oz) white wine	Fresh chervil sprigs, to garnish

Method

1

In a bowl, mix together the flour, 5 ml (1 tsp) salt and the eggs with your fingers to form a dough. Shape into a ball.

2

Divide the dough into 4 and flatten each piece before passing it through the rollers of a pasta machine.

3

Continue rolling until long, thin strips of pasta are formed. Flour frequently during the process.
Cut into small rectangles and leave to dry for 2 hours.

4

Cook the lasagne sheets a few at a time in a pan of boiling salted water, with 15 ml (1 tbsp) oil added,
for 3 minutes per batch.

5

Remove and refresh with cold water, then lay on a damp tea-towel until required.

6

Wash and scrub the cockles and mussels thoroughly. Shell the prawns and cut into pieces. Set aside.

7

Pour the wine into a flameproof casserole dish, add the shallots and cockles and cook, covered, over a high heat
until opened. Remove. Cook the mussels in the same liquid until opened. Remove and discard the shells from both,
and reserve the cooking liquid.

8

Fry the onion and garlic in the remaining 45 ml (3 tbsp) oil in a frying pan. Add the tomatoes and 15 ml (1 tbsp) parsley.
Strain the stock from the shellfish through a sieve lined with muslin.

9

Add the prawns, cockles and mussels with their cooking liquid to the pan. Cook over a moderate
heat for 20 minutes, stirring occasionally.

10

Brush an ovenproof baking dish with some of the butter. Layer the sheets of lasagne with the seafood mixture, brushing
the pasta with butter each time. Finish with a layer of lasagne and brush with butter.
Cover with foil and bake in a preheated oven at 200°C/400°F/Gas Mark 6 for 25-30 minutes.

11

Remove the foil and brown the top of the lasagne under a preheated grill for 5 minutes.
Serve, cut into portions, garnished with the chervil sprigs.

Serving suggestion

Serve with fresh crusty French bread and a mixed green side salad.

Shrimps with Plantain

This exotic dish features a combination of shrimps and plantain, or 'cooking bananas' as they are often known, flavoured with curry spices.

Preparation time: 10 minutes • Cooking time: 25-30 minutes • Serves: 4-6

Ingredients

1 kg (2 lb 4 oz) ripe plantains	125 ml (4 fl oz) hot stock
20 g (¾ oz) butter	125 ml (4 fl oz) milk
2 large onions, finely chopped	400 g (14 oz) shelled shrimps
2 bay leaves	Lemon juice
30 ml (2 tbsp) curry powder	Salt and freshly ground black pepper

Method

1
Peel the plantains and cut into 1-cm (½-in) slices.

2
Melt the butter in a pan and cook the onions until softened, stirring occasionally, then add the plantains, bay leaves and curry powder.

3
Stir and cook for about 1 minute. Pour in the hot stock, cover the pan and simmer for about 10 minutes, stirring occasionally.

4
Add the milk, then cook, uncovered, for a further 10 minutes, stirring occasionally.

5
Heat the shrimps through in the sauce for about 1 minute, adding lemon juice and salt and pepper to taste. Remove the bay leaves and serve.

Serving suggestions
Serve with boiled rice and a chopped side salad or fresh cooked mixed vegetables.

Variations
Use ripe mango or pineapple in place of plantains. Use small prawns or cooked, shelled mussels in place of shrimps.

Cook's tip
Plantains or cooking bananas have a delicate sweet taste and are slightly floury when ripe. They combine well with pork and chicken as well as shellfish.

Haddock in Mustard Sauce

The creamy mustard-flavoured sauce in this recipe adds a touch of richness and spice to plainly cooked haddock.

Preparation time: 10 minutes • Cooking time: 30 minutes • Serves: 4

Ingredients

250 ml (9 fl oz) dry white wine	1 egg yolk
1 bay leaf	30 ml (2 tbsp) milk or cream
A pinch of dried thyme	30 ml (2 tbsp) mustard
5 ml (1 tsp) salt	40 g (1½ oz) butter
10 peppercorns	Freshly ground white pepper
4 x 175-g (6-oz) haddock cutlets or fillets	Sugar, to taste
125 g (4½ oz) crème fraîche	Chopped fresh parsley, to sprinkle
15-30 ml (1-2 tbsp) plain flour	Lemon slices and tomato slices, to garnish

Method

1
In a saucepan, bring the wine and 125 ml (4 fl oz) water to the boil with the bay leaf, thyme, salt and peppercorns.

2
Add the fish to the liquid and simmer for about 20 minutes, until cooked and tender.

3
Using a spatula, place the fish on a warmed dish, cover and keep warm in a low oven.

4
For the mustard sauce, strain the fish stock, retaining 250 ml (9 fl oz) liquid. Bring to the boil in a pan.

5
Mix the crème fraîche with the flour in a bowl and gradually stir into the fish stock.

6
Cook gently for about 5 minutes, stirring, then mix the egg yolk with the milk or cream and mustard. Add to the pan, stirring.

7
Stir in the butter and season with pepper and sugar to taste.

8
Sprinkle the fish with chopped parsley, garnish with lemon and tomato slices and serve with the sauce spooned over.

Serving suggestion
Serve with croquette or sautéed potatoes, mangetout and baby corn.

Variations
Use wholegrain mustard if you like. Use other white fish such as cod or plaice.

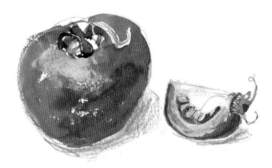

Baked Sardines

A simple yet delicious dish of fresh sardines oven-baked with garlic and herbs.

Preparation time: 10 minutes • Cooking time: 20 minutes • Serves: 6

Ingredients

1.25 kg (2 lb 12 oz) whole sardines	*4 cloves garlic, crushed*
1 lemon, sliced	*30 ml (2 tbsp) chopped fresh parsley*
1 tomato, sliced	*Salt and freshly ground black pepper*
Juice of 1 lemon	*15 ml (1 tbsp) chopped fresh marjoram*
75 ml (5 tbsp) olive oil	

Method

1
Place the sardines next to each other in a greased shallow ovenproof dish.

2
Arrange the slices of lemon and tomato between the fish.

3
Mix the lemon juice with the oil and drizzle the mixture over the fish.

4
Sprinkle the garlic over the fish with the parsley, salt and pepper and marjoram.

5
Bake in a preheated oven at 200°C/400°F/Gas Mark 6 for about 20 minutes, until the fish
are cooked and tender. Serve immediately.

Serving suggestion
Serve with baked potatoes and a tomato, onion and pepper salad.

Variations
Use small mackerel in place of sardines. Use lime juice in place of lemon juice. Use oregano in place of marjoram.

Salt Cod with Peppers

This dish is based on a traditional Portuguese country recipe using potato, cod and tomato. It has been modernised and refined in an elegant preparation of layered puréed potato, cod and ratatouille.

Preparation time: 1 hour 40 minutes, plus 24 hours soaking time • Cooking time: 30 minutes • Serves: 6

Ingredients

1 kg (2 lb 4 oz) salt cod	*6 cloves garlic, chopped*
5 large potatoes	*1 small red chilli, seeded and chopped*
3 large onions, finely chopped	*2 red peppers, seeded and sliced*
45 ml (3 tbsp) olive oil	*2 green peppers, seeded and sliced*
60 ml (4 tbsp) double cream	*2 tomatoes, skinned, seeded and chopped*
30 ml (2 tbsp) chopped fresh parsley	*Fresh chervil sprigs, to garnish*
Salt and freshly ground black pepper	

Method

1

Cut the salt cod into small pieces. Soak in a bowl of water for 24 hours, changing the water several times.

2

Peel the potatoes, cut into quarters and cook in a pan of boiling, salted water with 1 chopped onion and 15 ml (1 tbsp) oil for 30 minutes, until tender.

3

Drain the potatoes and onions. Blend until smooth in a food processor or blender, or press through a sieve into a bowl. Add the cream and parsley and season to taste. Set aside.

4

Place the soaked and drained cod in a pan with a large amount of water. Bring to the boil and cook for 5 minutes.

5

Set aside to drain and cool, then flake the fish with your fingers, discarding the skin and bones.

6

Heat the remaining oil in a pan, add the garlic and chilli and cook until softened and lightly coloured, stirring occasionally.

7

Add the peppers and the remaining onions and cook for 10 minutes over a moderate heat, stirring frequently.

8

Add the tomatoes to the pan and cook for a further 15 minutes, stirring frequently.

9

Grease the bottom of an ovenproof dish. Spread the potato purée over the bottom, then spread over the cod. Top with the pepper, onion and tomato mixture.

10

Bake in a preheated oven at 200°C/400°F/Gas Mark 6 for 30 minutes. Serve hot, garnished with the chervil sprigs.

Serving suggestion

Serve with mixed cooked fresh vegetables such as baby carrots, sweetcorn and shredded green cabbage.

Variations

Use 4 leeks in place of onions. Use dill or tarragon in place of parsley. Use sweet potatoes in place of standard potatoes.

Monkfish and Pepper Kebabs

Monkfish is ideal for making kebabs since it can be cut into firm cubes that do not disintegrate during cooking.

Preparation time: 30 minutes • Cooking time: 25 minutes • Serves: 4

Ingredients

8 rashers of lean bacon, rind removed	*45 ml (3 tbsp) vegetable oil*
450 g (1 lb) monkfish, skinned and cut into 2.5-cm (1-in) pieces	*125 ml (4 fl oz) dry white wine*
	60 ml (4 tbsp) tarragon vinegar
1 small green pepper, seeded and cut into 2.5-cm (1-in) pieces	*2 shallots, finely chopped*
	15 ml (1 tbsp) chopped fresh tarragon
1 small red pepper, seeded and cut into 2.5-cm (1-in) pieces	*15 ml (1 tbsp) chopped fresh chervil or parsley*
12 small mushroom caps	*225 g (8 oz) butter, softened*
8 bay leaves	*Salt and freshly ground black pepper*

Method

1

Cut the bacon rashers in half lengthways, then again in half crossways.

2

Place a piece of the fish onto each piece of bacon and roll the bacon around the fish.

3

Thread the bacon and fish rolls onto large skewers, alternating with slices of pepper, mushroom and bay leaves.

4

Brush the kebabs with oil and arrange on a grill pan.

5

Preheat the grill to hot and cook the kebabs for 10-15 minutes, turning frequently to prevent the kebabs from over-cooking.

6

Meanwhile, heat the wine, vinegar and shallots in a small saucepan until boiling. Cook rapidly to reduce by half.

7

Add the herbs and lower the heat.

8

Using a fork or small whisk, beat the butter bit by bit into the hot wine mixture, whisking rapidly until the sauce becomes thick. Season to taste with salt and pepper.

9

Arrange the kebabs on a serving plate and serve with a little of the sauce spooned over and the remainder in a separate jug.

Serving suggestion
Serve with boiled rice and a mixed garden salad.

Variations
Use cod or haddock in place of monkfish. Use coriander in place of tarragon. Use baby corn, halved, in place of mushrooms.

Cook's tip
When making the sauce, it is important to whisk briskly, or it will not thicken sufficiently.

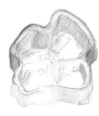

Scallops à la Nage with Leeks and Truffles

This is a rich and expensive dish – guaranteed to make a memorable meal.

Preparation time: 35 minutes • Cooking time: 20 minutes • Serves: 6

Ingredients

18 scallops, in their shells	*Salt and freshly ground black pepper*
3 medium leeks	*2 truffles, brushed clean*
25 g (1 oz) butter	*200 ml (7 fl oz) double cream*
250 ml (9 fl oz) fish stock	*Chopped fresh herbs (chervil or chives), to garnish*

Method

1

Open the scallops using the tip of a sharp knife and prise off the top shells. Slip the knife in under the scallops and cut from their shells.

2

Remove the fleshy 'bearded' parts from around the scallops and discard. Reserve the corals for another dish.

3

Rinse the scallops, removing all the sand and grit. Dry on a clean tea-towel.

4

Trim the roots from the leeks, then cut into 4 lengthways. Wash thoroughly and finely shred.

5

Melt the butter in a deep saucepan and add the leeks. Cook, stirring, for 1 minute.

6

Pour over the stock, season with salt and pepper and simmer for 15 minutes, stirring occasionally.

7

Slice the scallops crossways in 2 or 3 pieces, then add to the saucepan. Cook for 1 minute.

8

Cut the truffles into even-sized rounds, then into very thin matchstick slices.

9

Add the cream, truffles and truffle juice to the leeks and scallops. Cook for 5 minutes, stirring occasionally.

10

Serve the scallops and sauce hot, garnished with the chopped herbs.

Serving suggestion

Serve with creamed potatoes, broccoli florets and baby carrots.

Variations

Use mussels in place of scallops. Use double or triple the quantity of mussels to scallops and cook in boiling water to open the shells, then remove from the shells.

Cook's tip

The costly truffles, found in speciality food stores, can be reduced in quantity or eliminated, since there is no substitute.

Lobster with Bananas

A quick and easy treat to enjoy with a special friend or partner.

Preparation time: 20 minutes • Cooking time: 3 minutes (microwave) • Serves: 2

Ingredients

2 bananas	45 ml (3 tbsp) tomato ketchup
Lemon juice	Tabasco sauce, to taste
250 g (9 oz) hot cooked rice	Sugar
5 ml (1 tsp) ground cinnamon	Salt
175 g (6 oz) canned lobster meat	Fresh herb sprigs, to garnish
100 g (3½ oz) canned shrimps	

Method

1

Peel the bananas and cut into thin slices. Sprinkle the banana slices with lemon juice.

2

Mix the bananas into the hot cooked rice in a bowl, together with the cinnamon. Set aside and keep hot.

3

Drain the lobster meat and shrimps. Place both in a microwave-proof dish with the tomato ketchup, 45 ml (3 tbsp) water, a little Tabasco and sugar and salt to taste.

4

Cover and cook in a microwave oven for 3 minutes on LOW/MEDIUM until hot.

5

Spoon the rice and banana mixture onto a warm serving dish and arrange the lobster and shrimps on top.

6

Garnish with herb sprigs and serve.

Serving suggestion

Serve with a mixed dark leaf salad and warm ciabatta bread.

Variations

Use 1-2 small ripe mangoes in place of bananas. Use chilli powder or curry powder in place of cinnamon. Use flaked crab or tuna in place of lobster.

Ocean Perch and King Prawn Duet

In this elegant dish, onions, peppers, courgette and tomato are slowly cooked, then puréed and topped with steamed fish and king prawns sautéed in olive oil.

Preparation time: 30 minutes • Cooking time: 35 minutes • Serves: 6

Ingredients

18 raw king prawns	1 courgette, sliced
800 g (1 lb 12 oz) ocean perch or cod fillets	1 tomato, skinned, seeded and chopped
75 ml (5 tbsp) olive oil	1 bouquet garni (parsley, thyme, bay leaf)
1 onion, finely chopped	Salt and freshly ground black pepper
½ red pepper, seeded and thinly sliced	250 ml (9 fl oz) fish stock
½ green pepper, seeded and thinly sliced	Fresh chervil, to garnish
1 clove garlic, finely chopped	

Method

1

Shell the prawns and remove and discard their heads and tails. Cut down the back of the prawns, devein, then cut in two lengthways. Set aside.

2

Cut the perch or cod fillets into even, bite-sized pieces and set aside.

3

Heat 45 ml (3 tbsp) oil in a pan and fry the onion and peppers for 3 minutes. Add the garlic, courgette and tomato pulp. Mix well and cook for 5 minutes, stirring occasionally.

4

Add the bouquet garni, salt and pepper to taste and stock. Cover and cook over a moderate heat for 20 minutes, stirring frequently.

5

Heat the remaining oil in a separate pan and sear the prawns evenly all over for 3 minutes. Season with salt and pepper. Drain on absorbent kitchen paper and keep warm in the oven.

6

Place the fish in a steamer. Season with salt and pepper and steam, covered, over a pan of boiling water for 5 minutes.

7

Remove and discard the bouquet garni from the vegetable mixture and blend to a smooth purée with a hand-held electric mixer.

8

Serve the cooked fish and prawns with the vegetable purée sauce, garnished with the fresh chervil.

Serving suggestion

Serve with minted boiled new potatoes and a selection of cooked baby vegetables.

Variations

Use haddock or monkfish in place of perch or cod. Use 1 parsnip in place of the courgette.
Use 1 red onion in place of standard onion.

Deep-Fried Seafood and Vegetables

This is a delicious and fun way to serve fresh seafood, vegetables and herbs.

Preparation time: 15 minutes, plus 15 minutes standing time • Cooking time: 10-12 minutes • Serves: 2-4

Ingredients

6-8 thin, baby carrots	250 ml (9 fl oz) Pilsener beer or lager
6-8 thin, baby parsnips	1 medium egg, beaten
2 fennel bulbs	Salt and freshly ground black pepper
4 large uncooked prawns	Vegetable oil, for deep-frying
200 g (7 oz) prepared squid	8 sprigs of fresh parsley
Lemon juice, for sprinkling	Lemon slices, to garnish
250 g (9 oz) plain flour	

Method

1

Remove all but 1-cm (½ in) of the foliage from the carrots, if they have any. Scrape both the carrots and the parsnips.

2

Slice the fennel bulbs into quarters.

3

Shell the prawns and cut the squid into rings. Sprinkle both with lemon juice, place in a dish and set aside for 15 minutes. Pat dry with absorbent kitchen paper.

4

Sift the flour into a bowl and make a well in the centre of the flour.

5

Pour some of the beer or lager into the well and mix together.

6

Add the remainder of the beer with the egg, and beat to form a smooth batter. Season to taste with salt and pepper.

7

Place the oil in a deep-fat fryer and heat to a temperature of 180°C/350°F. Dip the vegetables, parsley and seafood in the batter and deep-fry in small portions until brown. Each portion of vegetables and sprig of parsley should cook for 3-5 minutes and the fish for 10-12 minutes.

8

Drain on absorbent kitchen paper and sprinkle with salt. Serve, garnished with slices of lemon.

Serving suggestions

Serve with oven-baked chips or sautéed potatoes and petit pois.

Variations

Use your own selection of prepared seafood, such as scallops and mussels. Use coriander in place of parsley.

Grilled Sea Bass with Fennel and Aniseed

Aniseed is a wonderfully aromatic flavouring for fish.

Preparation time: 40 minutes plus 1 hour marinating time • Cooking time: 30 minutes • Serves: 6

Ingredients

6 small sea bass, filleted	2 shallots, finely chopped
Salt and freshly ground black pepper	2 tomatoes, skinned, seeded and chopped
Juice of ½ lemon	300 ml (½ pint) fish stock
15 ml (1 tbsp) aniseed	200 ml (7 fl oz) double cream
45 ml (3 tbsp) olive oil	30 ml (2 tbsp) butter
500 ml (18 fl oz) milk	Fresh dill sprigs, to garnish
3 fennel bulbs, sliced	

Method

1

Cut each sea bass fillet in two, to obtain 4 small fillets per person. Season with salt and pepper and set aside.

2

In a bowl, mix together the lemon juice, aniseed and 30 ml (2 tbsp) oil. Add the fish fillets and leave to marinate for 1 hour, turning occasionally.

3

Bring the milk to a boil in a saucepan. Add a little salt and the fennel slices and cook for 5 minutes. Drain, then spread out to dry on a clean tea-towel.

4

Drain the fish marinade into a frying pan. Add the shallots and tomatoes and cook for 3 minutes, then add the stock. Reduce over a high heat for 5 minutes, stirring occasionally.

5

Add the cream and bring to the boil. Remove from the heat and blend until smooth with a hand-held electric mixer. Check the seasoning.

6

Strain the sauce through a fine sieve, pressing through with a spoon to obtain a smooth texture. Keep warm in a bowl over a pan of boiling water.

7

Preheat a cast-iron griddle and grease with the remaining oil. Sear the fish fillets on each side, then place in an ovenproof dish and finish cooking in a preheated oven at 200°C/400°F/Gas Mark 6 for 10 minutes.

8

Meanwhile, cook the fennel in the butter in a pan until lightly coloured, stirring occasionally. Season with salt and pepper.

9

To serve, top the fennel with the fish and sauce. Garnish with dill sprigs.

Serving suggestion

Serve with minted boiled new potatoes and grilled mixed vegetables such as peppers and courgettes.

Variations

Use trout in place of sea bass. Use 1 small onion in place of the shallots. Use lime juice in place of lemon juice.

Spiced King Prawns

Fresh prawns are served with a creamy, aromatic sauce for a celebration starter.

Preparation time: 10 minutes • Cooking time: 15 minutes • Serves: 2-4

Ingredients

20 g (³/₄ oz) butter	125 ml (4 fl oz) white wine
4 spring onions, sliced into rings	Salt and freshly ground white pepper
12 fresh uncooked king prawns	200 g (7 oz) crème fraîche
5 ml (1 tsp) ground cumin	15 ml (1 tbsp) chopped pine nuts
5 ml (1 tsp) ground coriander	

Method

1
Melt the butter in a pan and cook the spring onions until softened, stirring occasionally.

2
Add the prawns and cook until they turn pink, stirring occasionally.

3
Remove from the heat, place on a plate and keep warm.

4
Sprinkle the ground spices into the pan and add the white wine.

5
Add salt and pepper to taste, then stir in the crème fraîche. Bring gently to the boil.

6
Return the prawns to the sauce, stir to mix, then serve sprinkled with pine nuts.

Serving suggestions
Serve on slices of toast for a starter or with spicy rice as a main dish.

Variations
Use 2 shallots in place of spring onions. Use 10 ml (2 tsp) chilli powder in place of cumin and coriander.
Use almonds in place of pine nuts.

Red Mullet with Nutmeg

For this original fish dish, courgette 'galettes' are prepared much like potato pancakes, then decoratively topped with sautéed fish fillets and served in a nutmeg-flavoured cream sauce.

Preparation time: 45 minutes • Cooking time: 50 minutes • Serves: 6

Ingredients

2 red mullet, weighing about 1 kg (2 lb 4 oz) each	100 ml (3½ fl oz) rich fish stock
8 courgettes	300 ml (½ pint) double cream
1 medium egg	1 nutmeg
15 ml (1 tbsp) crème fraîche	½ lemon
Salt and freshly ground black pepper	30 ml (2 tbsp) butter
75 ml (5 tbsp) olive oil	½ bunch of fresh chives, chopped

Method

1
Cut the fins off the red mullet with a pair of scissors. Scrape off the scales with a fish scaler or the blade of a sharp knife. Gut, if not already done, and rinse well.

2
With a sharp knife, cut off the fillets, running the knife carefully down the backbone. Set aside.

3
Using a vegetable grater, grate the courgettes into thin julienne (matchsticks). Discard the soft seedy centre.

4
In a bowl, beat the egg with the crème fraîche and salt and pepper to taste, then add the courgettes. Mix thoroughly with a fork.

5
In a small ovenproof frying pan, heat 15 ml (1 tbsp) of the oil and fry ⅓ of the courgette mixture, flattening it into a pancake shape.

6
After about 3 minutes, turn over the courgette galette, then finish cooking in a preheated oven at 200°C/400°F/Gas Mark 6 for 5-10 minutes. Repeat the process two more times using the remaining courgette mixture and 30 ml (2 tbsp) oil. Set aside and keep warm.

7
In a saucepan, reduce the stock by half by boiling rapidly, then stir in the double cream, 6 or 7 gratings of nutmeg and salt and pepper to taste. Boil for 1 minute.

8
Remove from the heat, blend until smooth with a hand-held electric mixer, then add a few drops of lemon juice and keep warm over a bowl of hot water.

9
Season the red mullet fillets with salt and pepper and a few gratings of nutmeg.

10
Heat the remaining 30 ml (2 tbsp) oil and the butter in a pan and fry the fish on both sides until lightly coloured. Finish cooking in the oven for 8 minutes.

11
Cut the courgette galettes into 8 pieces, spread the pieces out on a plate, lay the fish over and pour over the sauce. Sprinkle over the chopped chives and serve.

Serving suggestion
Serve with croquette potatoes, petit pois and carrots.

Variations
Use parsnips in place of courgettes. Use vegetable stock in place of fish stock. Use parsley in place of chives.

Rice Pilaf with Mixed Seafood

In this appetising dish, rice is cooked pilaf style in a seafood stock, then mixed with a variety of seafood and a creamy herb sauce.

Preparation time: 45 minutes • Cooking time: 40 minutes • Serves: 6

Ingredients

2 shallots, sliced crossways	150 g (5½ oz) mushrooms, thinly sliced
6 large clams, well washed, in their shells	600 g (1 lb 5 oz) long-grain rice
250 ml (9 fl oz) white wine	Fish stock
1 litre (1¾ pints) mussels, in their shells, well washed	Salt and freshly ground black pepper
500 g (1 lb 2 oz) cockles, in their shells, well washed	250 ml (9 fl oz) double cream
12 clams, in their shells, well washed	5 sprigs of fresh parsley, finely chopped
40 g (1½ oz) butter	Fresh herbs, to garnish

Method

1
In a frying pan, cook the shallots with the large clams and white wine, covered, until the clams open.

2
Remove the clams and set aside, leaving the liquid in the pan. Add the mussels and cook, covered, until the shells open.

3
Remove the mussels and set aside, then add the cockles and cook, covered, until the shells open.

4
Remove the cockles and cook the small clams, covered, in the same liquid until open.

5
Remove the shellfish from their shells. Cut out the intestinal bags from the larger shellfish, if necessary. Rinse well to eliminate any sand or grit.

6
Strain the cooking liquid through a muslin-lined sieve, discard the residue and set aside the stock.

7
In a flameproof, ovenproof frying pan, heat the butter and fry the shellfish, mushrooms and rice, shaking the pan continuously. Cook for 2 minutes over a high heat.

8
Pour into the frying pan fish stock 1½ times the volume of the rice. Season, cover and cook in a preheated oven at 220°C/425°F/Gas Mark 7 for 25 minutes.

9
In a small pan, reduce the cooking liquid from the shellfish for 1 minute over a medium heat. Add the cream and reduce for a further 2 minutes. Blend the mixture with a hand-held electric mixer until smooth, then add the chopped parsley.

10
Serve the rice and shellfish in a mound with the sauce poured around the edge. Garnish with fresh herbs.

Serving suggestion
Serve with cooked fresh vegetables such as carrots, broccoli and cauliflower.

Variations
Use fresh coriander in place of parsley. Use crème fraîche in place of double cream. Use courgettes in place of mushrooms.

Cook's tip
The different varieties of seafood can be varied according to your taste and the availability of fresh ingredients.

Lemon Sole Roulades in a White Wine Sauce

These impressive fish rolls are served with prawns in a rich, creamy sauce.

Preparation time: 15 minutes • Cooking time: 20 minutes • Serves: 4

Ingredients

8 lemon sole fillets, weighing about 600 g (1 lb 5 oz) in total	100 g (3½ oz) cooked, shelled prawns
60 ml (4 tbsp) lemon juice	125 ml (4 fl oz) double cream
200 ml (7 fl oz) white wine	2 egg yolks
200 ml (7 fl oz) stock	Freshly ground white pepper
10 g (¼ oz) butter	Fresh watercress sprigs, lemon slices and red pepper strips, to garnish
5 ml (1 tsp) salt	

Method

1

Sprinkle the fillets of fish with lemon juice, roll up and secure with cocktail sticks.

2

In a saucepan, bring the wine, stock, butter and salt to the boil, add the sole roulades and cook for about 12 minutes.

3

Just before the fish is fully cooked, add the prawns to heat through. Remove the fish and prawns from the stock, place on a plate, cover and keep warm.

4

Boil the stock rapidly to reduce to about ⅓ its original volume, then whisk in the cream and egg yolks.

5

Remove the sauce from the heat and season with salt and pepper to taste.

6

Serve the roulades and prawns with the sauce poured over. Garnish with watercress sprigs, lemon slices and red pepper strips.

Serving suggestion

Serve with boiled new potatoes, mangetout and asparagus.

Variations

Use plaice in place of sole. Use crab meat or salmon (flaked) in place of prawns. Use crème fraîche in place of cream.

Index